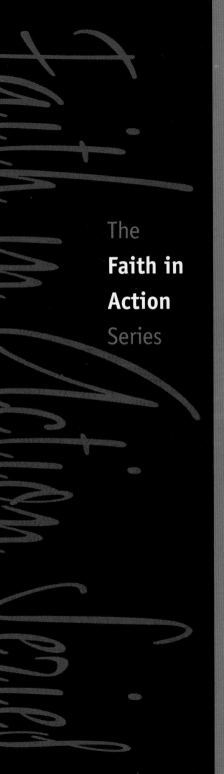

The
Faith in
Action
Series

Daring to Do What is Right

The Story of Dietrich Bonhoeffer

Terence Copley

Illustrated by Paul Bryn Davies

RMEP

RELIGIOUS AND MORAL EDUCATION PRESS

DARING TO DO WHAT IS RIGHT

The Story of Dietrich Bonhoeffer

One grey early morning, 9 April 1945, sentence of death was read out to a prisoner. He had arrived by lorry at the Nazi concentration camp at Flossenbürg in Bavaria, Germany, during the previous night. There was no right of appeal and no waiting time.

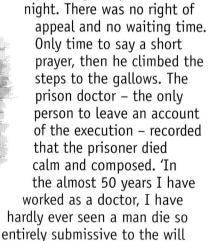

Only time to say a short prayer, then he climbed the steps to the gallows. The prison doctor – the only person to leave an account of the execution – recorded that the prisoner died calm and composed. 'In the almost 50 years I have worked as a doctor, I have hardly ever seen a man die so entirely submissive to the will of God.'

The executed man was called Dietrich Bonhoeffer. He was a Christian pastor (in some churches he might be called a priest or minister or vicar), aged 39. He was not hanged on the charge of being a Christian, but for being part of a plot to kill Hitler. Both were true – Bonhoeffer *was* a Christian leader *and* he was involved with a group who plotted to kill Hitler.

How had this all come about?

Bonhoeffer the boy

Dietrich Bonhoeffer had a twin sister called Sabine. They were born on 4 February 1906 in Breslau. There were six other children. Their father, Karl Bonhoeffer, was professor of psychiatry at the University of Berlin. Karl was a quiet man who spoke with authority and expected his children to be respectful – but at the same time he wanted them to think for themselves. Dietrich's mother, Paula, was lively, imaginative, energetic and deeply Christian. She wanted her children to become responsible adults. They lived in a Berlin suburb, home of many professors and senior university staff.

Dietrich's grandmother Julie (who died aged 94 in 1936)

opposed the Nazis from the beginning and strode between the guards who were trying to stop people using Jewish shops in the 1930s – so she too was very strong-minded. The other grandmother, Clara, was a countess who was very musical. This love of music was passed down the family. Each child learned an instrument and Saturday evening (pre-television and computer games, of course) was a family musical evening.

Bonhoeffer family entertainment

Paula's father, Karl-Alfred (Dietrich's grandfather), a preacher at the court of the Kaiser Wilhelm II, was not afraid to speak out either. He criticised the Kaiser publicly for referring to the ordinary people as 'rabble'. Karl-Alfred got into a lot of trouble for this. So the Bonhoeffer home was a place where education, independent-mindedness and speaking out, alongside politeness and respect, were all valued and encouraged. The Bonhoeffers were well off but the children were not spoilt and they had to give an account to Karl every week of how they spent their pocket-money.

The First World War (1914–18) touched the family when Dietrich's brother Walter was killed in 1917. Afterwards, when Dietrich was about 15, he started to think about the study of theology and about working for the Lutheran Church as a minister. Karl, not an enthusiastic Christian, thought life as a minister might be boring, so he was not excited about this as a career for his son, but true to his beliefs about independence, he wanted Dietrich to make up his own mind. Karl-Friedrich – another brother – was an atheist who became a professor of physics, so there was plenty of discussion about religion and other controversial issues in the Bonhoeffer home. When Dietrich the boy was not studying or sharing in the social life of the family, he enjoyed playing chess, ice skating, and acting in and producing amateur dramatics.

What Do You Think?

Important: In answering 'What Do You Think?' questions in this book, it is important that you not only state your opinion but also give as many reasons as possible for your opinion.

1. What are the key ingredients of a good upbringing? Make a list. Is there such a thing as the 'perfect childhood'? Explain your ideas fully. What effect do you think Bonhoeffer's upbringing might have had on his personality? (Might he feel strongly supported, perhaps under pressure to achieve, etc?)

2. Think about the qualities someone would need to cope with a lot of time on their own. How far do you think Bonhoeffer's childhood had prepared him for this? What special qualities might be needed to help someone to cope with a period of imprisonment?

Bonhoeffer the young man

After a year at the University of Tübingen, Bonhoeffer moved to the University of Berlin in 1924. Here he studied philosophy and church history. A visit to Rome, an 18th birthday present from his parents, made him realise that the world church was a lot bigger and more varied than his own German Lutheran church. He saw the Roman Catholic Church as a world church, embracing lots of cultures and ethnic groups and not just a one-country church.

Bonhoeffer completed his studies for a PhD (Doctor of Philosophy degree) in 1927 at the age of 21 – so he became 'Dr Bonhoeffer' at a very young age. Almost immediately he moved to Barcelona and spent two years as assistant pastor, helping to look after a congregation of about 200 German business people who were working in Spain. In one sermon he declared:

> *God wanders among us in human form, speaking to us in those who cross our paths, be they stranger, beggar, sick ...*

The port of Barcelona contained a large number of poor outsiders and it was Bonhoeffer's first real contact with people who were 'down and out'. He did not realise at this time that he would later become in some ways an outsider in his own country, eventually praying for its defeat in the Second World War.

After a brief return to Germany in which he passed his final examinations for the clergy, he moved to New York's Union Theological Seminary for a year's studentship until he reached the minimum age (25) to be a full pastor in the Lutheran Church in Germany. In New York Bonhoeffer met two issues he had not seen before: racism against black people and the question of pacifism. He spent most Sundays at the Abyssinian Baptist Church in Harlem. The injustice suffered by black people made Bonhoeffer angry with some white churches, which seemed to be telling black people to put up with their problems, suffer patiently and hope that 'one day' things would get better. To him, this was not living in the spirit of Jesus, but more like using religion as an excuse for doing nothing.

But it was clear to him that the situation of the Jews in Nazi Germany was becoming worse than that of African Americans. For Bonhoeffer the teaching of Jesus meant that all women and men are brothers and sisters, equal in God's sight. Given that humankind should be one family, it seemed absurd to Bonhoeffer that people who called themselves Christians should become involved in killing other people to extend their country's territory. He disliked the way in which some films made war and killing look exciting, glamorous, an adventure. He thought a lot about Jesus' words, 'But I say to you, love your enemies and pray for those who persecute you' (Matthew 5:44). How far should one take this?

Meeting the 'down and outs'

What Do You Think?

1. What do you think it means for 'God to wander among us in human form'?

2. What do you think 'the world church' started to mean to Bonhoeffer? What does the phrase mean to you?

3. The word 'pastor' really means shepherd. Why do you think that the Lutheran Church and some other churches use this word to describe their professional ministers?

4. Do you think religions should teach people to put up with the wrongs that are done to them rather than resist them?

5. If you were a Christian, how far would you take Jesus' words quoted above?

The rise of Nazism in Germany

'Nazi' is an abbreviation of NAtional SoZIalist German Workers Party. Despite the word 'socialist', which usually refers to left-wing parties, this party was extremely right wing. In the early 1920s Germany experienced one of the most severe price inflations of all time. One estimate puts it at 3.25 *million* per cent between 1920 and 1923. At its worst, in the second half of 1923, many prices rose more than five times every *week*. One US dollar ($1) was worth 2.5 *billion* Reichsmarks (German currency at the time). Some people's life savings ended up being worth the price of a loaf of bread. In 1924 Hitler, who was in prison at the time for attempting to seize power, started to write his book *Mein Kampf* (*My Struggle*). He wanted to restore Germany to greatness – but he had other ideas as well. He wanted to reduce crime, to help family life, to create full employment, build better roads, to reduce inflation – the sorts of things any politician might want to do in a country that was full of problems. But behind this list of good intentions was the desire to get votes so that he could become a dictator and put into action the darker plans he did *not* speak about as much. These included the plan to crush the Jewish population and to attack other groups – gay people, gypsies, communists, Jehovah's Witnesses, etc. Support for Nazism steadily grew, partly because people wanted jobs and a better standard of living and partly because they thought the country needed a very strong leader to get it out of the mess. The year 1933 was a key year for Germany and illustrates how successfully the Nazis took control.

In 1935 Jews lost the right to vote – but in 1942 after the Wannsee conference, the 'Final Solution' deprived them even of the right to live. How did the Nazis get away with it? It wasn't obvious that all this was happening. An American journalist, who, visited Germany in 1934, wrote about life at the time:

> In the background ... there lurked the terror of the Gestapo and the fear of the concentration camp ... Yet Nazi terror in the early years affected the lives of relatively few Germans ... [Nazism gave people] a new hope and a new confidence and an astonishing faith in the future of their country.
>
> William L. Shirer, *The Rise and Fall of the Third Reich*

Most people wanted to get on with their lives and didn't ask questions. It was always easier to look the other way. This was the background against which Bonhoeffer was developing his views and his career.

What Do You Think?

1. Is there a difference between a strong leader and a good leader? Link your answer to Hitler.

2. Should politicians have the right to control education? Give your reasons. Do the people who control our curriculum make some subjects more important than others? If so, are they right to do this?

3. The Nazis reduced the time given to Religious Education because they thought that religious teaching might attack what they were doing. In a group, discuss which particular religious teachings might have criticised the Nazis. Think of the Ten Commandments to begin with, but draw on material from any religion you know about.

4. Why was it 'always easier to look the other way'? What would have been the risks in *not* looking the other way?

1933

In 1933 Hitler became President and Chancellor of Germany, uniting the two most powerful political posts in the country. He gave immediate orders for the nazification of the school curriculum, for example one Reception class textbook had a cartoon of a Jew on the cover and the title 'Trust no Jew on his oath'. Racism – the idea of superior and inferior races – was taught through Nazi biology. History lessons became the glorious story of the Nazis. A new subject, 'Germanics', was invented, about the greatness of the so-called Master Race. Sport and toughness were emphasised. Girls were taught to be good wives and mothers. Anything like women's rights was forbidden. Religious Education was reduced in its timetable time and public examinations in RE (their version of the GCSE) were cancelled. At the same time, the State took control of the radio and the newspapers. A month later, Hitler was given 'emergency powers', including the power to arrest

Young school-children learning the Nazi salute

opponents to 'protect' them. Three internment (or 'concentration' camps) were opened to house them. Within another month, a boycott of Jewish businesses began and Jews were banned by law from state jobs. The Gestapo (secret police) was formed.

Other events quickly followed the Nazi take-over: trade unions were banned; Jewish, communist and other books felt to be 'anti-Nazi' were burned in public. Compulsory euthanasia was made legal for the mentally ill and for 'biologically inferior people' (the disabled, but also for other races). 'German Christians', a group of Nazis who claimed to be Christian, took over the top church jobs. Swastika flags appeared in many churches. After the death of President Hindenburg, Hitler declared himself *Führer* and abolished the post of President. He now had total political power. All this had happened in eight months in 1933.

Bonhoeffer the university lecturer

Bonhoeffer returned to Germany in 1931 to become a lecturer at the University of Berlin. Here he stood out for his independence of outlook – learned in childhood. Those students who were not attracted to the rapidly rising Nazi party and its views liked to attend his lectures because of their freshness and difference from official Nazi thinking. His students were among the fewer and fewer opponents of Nazism in the mid-1930s. Bonhoeffer made them think about peace by stating that war makes people blind to God. He added to his university lecturing by working as a chaplain at a technical university and accepting the leadership of a confirmation class of 50 boys in an extremely difficult and 'run down' area of Berlin. At first Bonhoeffer could barely keep order in the classes as the boys were so disruptive. He moved into the area, visited the boys' families, gave them Christmas presents, taught them English and took groups of boys who had never left the city on country holidays. The emphasis in Bonhoeffer's confirmation class was that Christianity is not a set of beliefs to be learned and recited at the confirmation service, but a community of people trying to live together with love and in the spirit of Jesus.

In 1931 he represented Germany at the World Alliance Conference of Churches in Cambridge. At this time co-operation between different Christian churches was not automatic but it was growing. Relationships between some churches had been bad and between others non-existent. Conferences in France, Switzerland and Czechoslovakia followed. Bonhoeffer was becoming known internationally and in Germany as a rising star in theology and in the Lutheran church.

But life wasn't all success. Bonhoeffer was turned down after his first application as parish minister as he was 'too young' and 'too outspoken'. The second job was lost when he withdrew his application to one of the big Berlin churches, as the church had accepted the Aryan

Boys' club group (Bonhoeffer back row, left)

clause, banning Jews and Jewish Christians – these were Christians who were also Jewish – from jobs. Bonhoeffer was not Jewish, but his good friend Pastor Franz Hildebrand was half Jewish and his twin sister Sabine had married into a family with Jewish connections. He disapproved strongly of anti-Semitism. So it was a matter of principle. He viewed it as more important than getting a good job.

Soon after Hitler achieved power as Chancellor, Bonhoeffer gave a live radio address in which he warned that with the dangerous cult of a dictator, the leader (*Führer*) could easily turn out to be a misleader (*Verführer*). He went on 'the leader who makes an idol of himself and his position makes a mockery of God'. The broadcast was cut off before he could get any further. Bonhoeffer was becoming known to the Nazis. In October 1933 he moved to London to become pastor of two small Lutheran churches, one in Sydenham and one in the East End. Here he tried to forget what was happening in Germany and the problem of deciding what to do to oppose it.

Back in Germany a group of churches came together as the Confessing Church (confession = an official statement of belief). They said: 'We reject the false teaching that there are areas of our life in which we do not belong to Jesus Christ but to other lords.' Guess who! It was very risky talk. In 1934 Bonhoeffer was invited by Gandhi to visit India. He wanted to go and study non-violent resistance, but an invitation came from the Confessing Church to return to Germany and work for them in training pastors

and representing the Church in international meetings. Bonhoeffer chose Germany, so once again he went home. He said that the churches working together internationally must halt the steps towards another world war. 'Peace on earth is not a problem but a commandment given at Christ's coming.'

What Do You Think?

1. Would it have been better if Bonhoeffer had spoken out less against Nazism (to draw less attention to himself) and concentrated more on secret resistance work?

2. In what ways might war make people 'blind to God'?

Bonhoeffer, resister of Nazism

The Nazis were now in control of all branches of German society, even the health service. Karl Bonhoeffer, Dietrich's father, was head of a psychiatric department in Berlin as well as professor. He chose to keep a number of Jewish assistants as staff, taking advantage of loopholes in the anti-Semitic laws to extend their contracts. In spite of his support, however, they eventually were sacked and had to emigrate. The Nazis also took over the Protestant churches. They either took over or closed down the church colleges for the training of pastors. Pro-Nazi and anti-Semitic teaching was given in the remaining colleges. In response, the Confessing Church decided to open a training centre at a former boarding school at Finkenwalde

near Stettin (Szczecin), close to the Polish border. It was a remote corner of Germany, now part of Poland, which helped the college to survive unnoticed by the Gestapo for two years. Bonhoeffer was appointed head of this college.

Daily life at Finkenwalde was simple. It included early rising, 30 minutes of silent meditation on a passage from the Bible, prayer, lectures, shared meals and providing help to local churches that had joined the Confessing Church. Finkenwalde taught and lived a strong sense of community – helping each other to try to lead a simple Christian life. Bonhoeffer's students were eager to attack the Nazi version of Christianity, but they were much less willing to attack Nazism itself. So was the wider Confessing Church, to Bonhoeffer's dismay. Open resistance to Nazism had become very dangerous. The very existence of Finkenwalde was an act of resistance, as it was illegal. But Bonhoeffer was later to go much further than this. In 1936 he was banned from lecturing at Berlin University. In 1937 Finkenwalde was closed down by the Gestapo. In 1938 all those involved as trainers of pastors in the Confessing Church were forbidden even to enter Berlin. This, of course, included Bonhoeffer. In the same year, the Nazi 'German Christians' insisted that all pastors should take a personal oath of allegiance to Hitler. Bonhoeffer campaigned vigorously against this. So by 1938 he was already under deep suspicion, especially as fewer people were speaking out against what was happening in Germany.

The year 1938 was eventful for other reasons. There was the Kristallnacht or Night of the Broken Glass attack on Jewish synagogues and homes on 9 November. Most Christians kept silent. But Bonhoeffer, who had underlined in his Bible Psalm 74 verse 8,

> *They burn all the houses of God in the land*

told his students 'if the synagogues are set on fire today, tomorrow the churches will burn'.

Some high-ranking members of the regular army – not the SS or the Gestapo – began to look for ways of removing Hitler from power. Bonhoeffer's brother-in-law, Hans von Dohnanyi, was involved in this plotting.

Synagogue burning on Kristallnacht

Hans von Dohnanyi

Bonhoeffer was his close friend. When Dohnanyi told him about it – in strict confidence – it made Bonhoeffer what is legally called an 'accessory before the fact'. In other words, he knew something was being planned against Hitler before it happened. The penalty even for this was death. It made him wonder whether it was necessary to start to work actively against the regime rather than just attack it with words. Bonhoeffer was soon to move from accessory to accomplice.

What Do You Think?

1. Are our modern lives too complicated? Compare them to life at Finkenwalde. Is it easier to live a simpler life if those around you are doing the same?

2. How far would you be prepared to go to stand up for what matters to you? Would you take a risk for the benefit of somebody else? Think of example(s).

3. Why did Bonhoeffer tell his students, 'If the synagogues are set on fire today, tomorrow the churches will burn'?

Bonhoeffer the conspirator

How could Bonhoeffer change from a near-pacifist position to one that supported violent action against Hitler? He told his sister-in-law Emmi:

> If I see a madman driving a car into a group of innocent bystanders, then I can't, as a Christian, simply wait for the catastrophe and then comfort the wounded and bury the dead. I must try to wrestle the steering wheel out of the hands of the driver.

It is hard to know exactly what Bonhoeffer knew about the various plans to assassinate Hitler, because for obvious reasons the plotters kept few written records and since those who were close to Bonhoeffer were executed, they could not tell their stories after the war. So this period of Bonhoeffer's life has parts we can't reconstruct. There had been plans to overthrow Hitler in 1938 and 1939 to stop him causing a war, but these came to nothing. After the start of war in 1939, Bonhoeffer returned from the USA, reducing a planned one-year visit to four weeks because he could not bear to be outside Germany in its time of trouble. He attended a secret meeting at Dohnanyi's house at which Joseph Müller, a secret agent, referred to the 'X report'. This was a record of negotiations with Britain and its allies to inquire whether they would be willing to come to peace with Germany if Hitler was first removed from power. Bonhoeffer also knew about a plan by Colonel Hans Oster to warn the Netherlands and Belgium about Germany's planned invasion. He also knew of plotting against Hitler by Admiral Canaris, who had witnessed SS attacks on Jews and was horrified. As a result, Canaris made contact with British Intelligence, MI6. But the rapid surrender of France in 1940 and Germany's other early victories in the war made Hitler look stronger than ever. The plotters were not a well-organised group and they lacked support both inside and outside Germany.

If Bonhoeffer knew a lot the Gestapo did not know, the Gestapo knew a lot about him. He continued to give illegal lectures in Berlin (see page 10) so in 1940 he was forbidden to speak in public anywhere on the grounds of 'subversive activity' and placed under orders to report regularly to the local police.

At this point, in a move to protect him, Dohnanyi and Oster arranged for him to become an unpaid agent for the Abwehr, the German Intelligence Service, headed by Canaris. The Abwehr quickly moved him from Berlin to work in their Munich office – ending daily reporting to the police – and Müller arranged for him to stay at Ettal Abbey, a Bavarian monastery, where he could write books when Abwehr work permitted, keep in touch with his ex-Finkenwalde students and with the conspirators. Even Ettal was not entirely safe. In 1938 every monk and all the pupils in the monastery school had been individually interrogated by members of the Gestapo. The abbot and two monks were arrested. During his arrest, one monk had been so savagely interrogated that he died after release.

Almost immediately after he arrived at Ettal, Bonhoeffer became involved in 'Operation 7', a daring scheme to smuggle

a group of seven Jews out of Germany into Switzerland under the pretence that they too were working for the Abwehr. Fake passports and genuine Swiss currency were arranged for them. Soon afterwards Bonhoeffer travelled to Norway to encourage Christian resistance to Nazism. Then he went to Sweden, officially on Abwehr business, but to meet the Church of England Bishop of Chichester, George Bell. He asked Bell to contact the British government to inquire whether, if Hitler were overthrown by the German resistance, Britain would be willing to make peace and quickly end the war. The reply came that only unconditional German surrender would be acceptable.

In the midst of this hectic life of travel and secrecy, Bonhoeffer's personal life did not stand still. In January 1943 he became engaged to Maria von Wedemeyer. She was highly intelligent and beautiful and came from a wealthy aristocratic family. He was 35. She was 18. He had known her and her family since she was 12, but the relationship only became more than friendship after she left school in the summer before their engagement. Much as he loved

Maria, he thought his life was too uncertain to make any plan to marry, but later he came to the view that life should be enjoyed, that love is a gift and that a marriage was possible. He later wrote to her:

> Our marriage shall be a yes to God's earth. I fear that Christians who stand with only one leg upon earth will also stand with only one leg in heaven.

What Do You Think?

1. What do you think Bonhoeffer meant by 'If I see a madman driving a car ...'?

2. Maria's family wanted the couple to have a long engagement before the wedding. Why do you think they asked for this?

3. Bonhoeffer was so opposed to Nazism that he wanted Germany to lose the war. How hard do you think it would be to wish and pray for your own country's defeat in a war?

4. What do you think Bonhoeffer meant by 'Christians who stand with only one leg' (above)?

Bonhoeffer the suspect

Such a well-known opponent of Nazism as Bonhoeffer could not escape Gestapo attention for long. By 1943 they were tapping the telephones of Bonhoeffer and Dohnanyi. In the spring two more plots against Hitler failed. It was as if he had a charmed life. On 13 March, Major General Tresckow and Lt von Schlabrendorff led what became known as 'Operation Flash'. An unsuspecting officer travelling with Hitler in his personal plane was asked to deliver a case containing 'two bottles of brandy' as a birthday present to someone at the destination. The 'present' was a time bomb. The British-made chemical pencil detonator on the bomb had been

tested many times and was considered reliable. It went off, but the bomb did not. When he heard the news, Tresckow rushed across with two real bottles of brandy and exchanged them for the bomb in order to avoid detection. On 21 March another attempt was made when Hitler visited an exhibition of captured Soviet weapons in Berlin. One of Tresckow's friends, Colonel von Gersdorff, volunteered to carry out a suicide bombing using the same bomb that had failed to go off on the plane, with a new detonator hidden on his body. But the only new fuse he could obtain was a ten-minute one. To everyone's surprise, Hitler left in less than ten minutes after hurrying past the display. Gersdorff – wearing the bomb that was about to blow him up – had to dash to a toilet to defuse it quickly to save his own life and prevent any suspicion of a plot. These conspirators could not know that a whole series of further attempts to kill Hitler would all fail. 'Luck' favoured Hitler again and again – it was credited to *'Vorsehung'*, Providence.

On 23 March 1943, Bonhoeffer was visiting his parents' home. He telephoned his sister Christina, Dohnanyi's wife. An unfamiliar man's voice answered the phone. Bonhoeffer immediately thought Hans von Dohnanyi had been arrested, or that the Gestapo were searching his house and not allowing him to take the call. Soon afterwards, a black Mercedes car pulled up outside the Bonhoeffer home. Bonhoeffer's father Karl answered the door. It was two members of the Gestapo asking to speak to Dietrich. Bonhoeffer was under arrest. The immediate reason was suspicion of involvement in Operation 7.

Bonhoeffer the prisoner

Imagine what it must have been like for Bonhoeffer to be arrested at all. Hardly by nature or upbringing a criminal, for Bonhoeffer to be taken away for questioning, possibly torture, with no clear idea of the charge or the date of any trial, must have been very frightening. He did not know how much or how little his captors knew about what he had been involved in. He was taken to the prison in Tegel, a suburb of Berlin. Here he was locked up alone. Some of the daily aspects of life – like soap and changes of clothing – were not immediately available. There were air raids on Berlin by British and US planes. Unlike other people, prisoners could not flee into shelters, which must have increased their fear. Bonhoeffer was also very worried that under clever interrogation, or physical torture, he might give away the names of other people who knew about the anti-Hitler plotting. Letters were censored – read by the prison authorities. His fiancée Maria was allowed to see him without any warning of her first visit, in the hope that he would reveal some secret as a result of surprise. But he was silent at first and only revealed his feelings by the squeeze he gave Maria's hand as he held it.

He had previously agreed a 'cover story' with Dohnanyi and Müller. They too were under arrest, in different prisons so they could not communicate. But with the help of smuggled letters and members of their families, limited communication was possible. Tegel was not a Gestapo prison or a concentration camp. Its staff included many soldiers sent back to Germany after being wounded in fighting on the Russian front. They were prepared to take letters out from the generous pastor and they relaxed the solitary confinement rule. Bonhoeffer was allowed books, coffee and special food sent by his family and by his fiancée Maria, even a few bottles of sparkling wine. Once Maria brought a Christmas tree. It was too big for his cell, but was placed in the

In Tegel prison

guards' office where he was allowed to visit it. He wrote poems, sketched ideas for novels and plays, read theological books, wrote about ideas for a different less churchy sort of church, where the pastors did ordinary jobs and the people were treated as full, independent adults and not just told to believe out of date or impossible things. But if there were some luxuries in prison, it was no holiday. Alongside this was the daily pressure of interrogation. He was questioned by a judge in the presence of a Gestapo official. Again and again they wanted to know about Dohnanyi. Their questioning lasted from April to June 1943. It gradually became clear that although his questioners suspected a lot – including his involvement in Operation 7 – they had no hard facts. All they knew was that he had avoided military service in the army – a serious offence – in order to join the Abwehr, which without Nazi permission did not count as military service. This alone was enough for a trial and from June 1943 onwards dates were set and reset until April 1944.

Things changed suddenly after 20 July 1944. In August 1943 Tresckow (see pages 13–14) met a young staff officer, Colonel Count Claus von Stauffenberg. Stauffenberg, a Roman Catholic, had at first welcomed Nazism but was disgusted by the systematic executions of Jewish civilians and the treatment of the Russian prisoners of war. From the beginning of 1942 he shared the widespread view among Army officers that Germany was being led to disaster and that Hitler must be removed from power. For some time Stauffenberg's religious beliefs prevented him from accepting assassination as a morally correct way to achieve this. After December 1942, when it was clear that Hitler intended the entire German Sixth Army to die rather than surrender at the Battle of Stalingrad, Stauffenberg came to the conclusion that *not* assassinating Hitler would be a greater moral evil. Combined casualties in this 199-day battle are estimated at above 1.5 million. The battle was marked by brutality and atrocities towards civilians and the wounded on both sides.

Other conspirators who had long resisted the idea of killing Hitler on moral grounds now changed their minds – partly because of hearing reports of mass murder at Auschwitz. On 20 July Stauffenberg flew back to Rastenburg for another Hitler military conference, with a bomb in his briefcase.

Despite Hitler's mania for security, officers attending his conferences were not searched. Stauffenberg entered the room and placed his briefcase bomb under the table around which Hitler and more than 20 officers were standing. After ten minutes Stauffenberg made an excuse and left the room. At 12.40p.m. the bomb went off, demolishing the conference room. Four people were seriously injured and died soon after. But Hitler survived, suffering only minor injuries. It is possible he had been saved because the briefcase had been moved behind the heavy oak leg of the conference table, which took

the force of the blast. By the end of the day Stauffenberg had been shot and other conspirators arrested.

Soon afterwards, the Gestapo discovered Canaris' secret files in a safe in the Abwehr emergency headquarters at Zossen. There was clear evidence against Dohnanyi, Bonhoeffer and others. Their execution was postponed by personal order of Hitler in order to allow the plot to be investigated thoroughly. So the failure of the 20 July 1944 plot – although Bonhoeffer was in prison at the time – directly led to his execution.

What Do You Think?

1. What can we deduce about Bonhoeffer's character from the way in which the guards treated him and how he chose to spend his time?

2. What sort of situation might force you to change some of your strongly held beliefs or principles?

3. Think about what is meant by 'the end justifies the means'. Does it? In what circumstances, if any?

Bonhoeffer at Tegel, 1944

Bonhoeffer, the end and the beginning

Bonhoeffer heard the news about the failed plot on the radio. He now knew that the outlook for him looked very bad. He wrote a poem, which began:

> Daring to do what is right, not what fancy may tell you,
> Valiantly grasping opportunities,
> Not doubting like a coward.
> Freedom comes only through actions, not through thoughts,
> Do not faint or fear, go out to the storm and the action,
> Trusting God ...

With the help of his family and a reliable guard, Bonhoeffer prepared to escape. The family smuggled in workman's clothing, money and food coupons and were waiting for a false passport to be made when Bonhoeffer's brother Klaus was arrested. This led Bonhoeffer to decide that if he did escape, the risk of Gestapo revenge arrests or punishment of members of his family or his fiancée for *Sippenhaft* (a law which held all members of a family responsible for the crime of one member) were high. He decided not to put them at risk by escaping. Soon afterwards he was transferred to the Gestapo prison in a Berlin basement. Escape was now impossible. There were no friendly guards. Conditions were worse and we cannot be sure what went on, or how 'severe' the interrogation was, as no outside communication was permitted. But he did manage snatched conversations with other plotters on the way from their cells to the showers and he seems to have been treated courteously in the hope that he would reveal more evidence against other plotters willingly.

What Do You Think?

1. Was Bonhoeffer right that 'Freedom comes only through actions, not through thoughts'? Give your reasons.

2. By not escaping, was Bonhoeffer right to put the safety of his family and fiancée above the cause he was fighting for? What might you have done?

3. What might have kept Bonhoeffer hoping even in the Gestapo prison? (Think of some religious and non-religious reasons for hoping.)

4. Do you think the saying 'Hope for the best, prepare for the worst' is good advice for people in any life-threatening situation (danger, serious illness, etc)?

What we know for sure is that Bonhoeffer was transferred to Buchenwald concentration camp on 7 February 1945, where he met British secret service Captain Payne Best, also a prisoner, whose account of Bonhoeffer's last months is all that survives. Here he was kept in a cellar outside the main camp with Müller and others. At Hitler's midday conference on 5 April 1945, the decision was taken to execute the 'Zossen group' (see page 17), which included Bonhoeffer. The group was to be transferred to Flossenbürg camp, but the lorry broke down near Schönberg and the prisoners were temporarily locked in a school. The order came from Berlin that

Bonhoeffer and others were to be 'tried' then executed. There was no jury and there was never a question of a not guilty verdict from the military judge. Bonhoeffer had just finished conducting a short Sunday service in the school when two men arrived to collect him. It was the Sunday after Easter. He was allowed to say goodbye to each of the others in the room. To Payne Best he gave a message to pass on to Bishop Bell in England:

> This is the end – for me, the beginning of life. Tell him [Bell] I believe in the principle of our universal Christian brotherhood, which rises above all nations.

The next morning, Bonhoeffer, Canaris, Oster and other 'Zossen conspirators' were executed.

Postscript

Dohnanyi was executed in Sachsenhausen concentration camp, probably on 9 April 1945. He had been severely tortured during interrogation. Flossenbürg camp was liberated by the US Army on 23 April 1945, less than three weeks after the executions. On 30 April 1945, less than four weeks after the executions, Hitler committed suicide. On 7 May 1945, just over a month after the executions, Germany surrendered and the war in Europe ended. Maria von Wedemeyer, Bonhoeffer's fiancée, emigrated to the USA after the war. She married there, worked as a computer systems analyst and died in 1977.

Maria von Wedemeyer

Biographical Notes

1906	Born in Breslau on 4 February, sixth of eight children. He was born before his twin sister.
1912	The family move to Berlin.
1917	Brother Walter killed in France in the First World War.
1923–4	Student at Tübingen, then Berlin.
1927	Receives doctorate (= advanced) degree. Dr B!
1928	Assistant pastor at Barcelona.
1930–31	Lives in New York for theological study.
1931	Becomes Lecturer at Berlin University. Represents Germany at the World Alliance Conference of Churches in Cambridge.
1933	Live radio broadcast warning of the dangers of a *Führer* is cut off. Becomes pastor of two Lutheran churches in London.
1934	Chooses to return to Germany rather than visit Gandhi in India.
1935	Accepts headship of an illegal college to train pastors in Finkenwalde.
1936	Banned from lecturing in Berlin.
1937	Publishes *The Cost of Discipleship*. Finkenwalde is closed down by the Gestapo.
1938	Contacts German resistance leaders.
1939	Visits England, then later returns from a planned one-year visit to the USA after only four weeks.
1940	Banned from all public speaking. Moves to Ettal monastery (Bavaria). Joins the Abwehr (German Military Intelligence) in their Munich office.
1941 and 1942	Visits Switzerland (neutral country) to hold meetings with conspirators and with British representatives like Bishop Bell.
1943	January: Becomes engaged to Maria von Wedemeyer. March: Karl Bonhoeffer gets the Goethe award for psychiatry for his 75th birthday. 5 April: In prison in Tegel.
1944	Transferred to the Gestapo prison in the basement of Prinz-Albrecht-Strasse, Berlin.
1945	7 February: Moved to Buchenwald concentration camp. 8 April: Moved to Flossenbürg concentration camp. 9 April: Executed.

Things to Do

1 In prison Bonhoeffer wrote these lines about prison life:

> *Separation from people*
> *From work*
> *From the past*
> *From the future*
> *From marriage*
> *From God.*

(a) Name three other key words (like *separation*) that might describe imprisonment.
(b) Choose one key word that might help a religious believer in prison and give your reasons.
(c) Write a short poem based on the key word you have chosen.

2 Ettal Abbey, Bavaria, was founded in 1330. It still exists.
(a) Find out from the Abbey's website about daily life there and what happened during the time of the Nazis. Describe it in your own words. (www.klaster-ettal.de/index-uk.html)
(b) Look at the photographs of it on the website and answer:
In what ways do you think that the buildings, the setting and the daily life of the monks at Ettal monastery might have helped Bonhoeffer, especially in his spiritual life, during the time he spent there?

3 While in Tegel prison, Bonhoeffer started a novel. In it appears this dialogue between a small boy and his grandma:

Boy: Is God very strict with people?
G'ma: Yes, God's very strict with us but also very good.
Boy: Do people always know they're going to die before they die?
[Bonhoeffer did not know that he would be one of these.]
G'ma: Not always but sometimes.
Boy: I want to know it before; then I'd hurry and do lots of good things so God would have to take me to heaven.
G'ma: God doesn't have to do anything, child. God does as God pleases.

(a) How well do you think the Grandma has answered the boy (assuming that God is real)?

(b) *Is* it an advantage to know when you're going to die? Give your reasons.

(c) If you were a Christian, would you feel that the disasters that overtook Germany were a sign of what the grandma calls God's strictness – a punishment?

4 Colonel Claus von Stauffenberg planned to be what we would now call a suicide bomber (see page 16). He was a Roman Catholic who had thought very carefully about what was involved. He was executed as soon as the plot was discovered. His wife Nina was arrested for *Sippenhaft* (see page 18), sent to a concentration camp (she survived, living until 2006) but their four children were taken into 'care' and forced to take new names as a warning that entire families would be punished.

(a) Try to argue the case from a Christian point of view that Stauffenberg was *wrong* to try to kill Hitler.

(b) Then write the answer that you think Bonhoeffer would have made to this argument.

(c) Imagine! You are Stauffenberg's Catholic priest and he tells you what he is planning to do the day before. What would you advise and why?

5 Postscript from Bonhoeffer's parents' last letter to him – they did not know where he had been moved from Berlin – 28 February 1945:

My thoughts are with you day and night. I'm worried how things may be going with you. I hope you can do some work and some reading and don't get too depressed. God help you and us through this difficult time.
Your old Mother
We are staying in Berlin come what may. (A reference to air raids and food shortages)

Knowing what you already do about Bonhoeffer's parents (see pages 2 and 3) but remembering that the letter would be read by a censor, draft the reply he might have written if he had received this. Then exchange your letter with someone else and read the other person's letter as a censor would. Does it give anything away that might be used against Bonhoeffer?

6 Jesus and Bonhoeffer both had in common that they were executed for a crime and not directly for religious reasons. (The Romans were not interested in the Jewish religious crime of blasphemy but probably executed Jesus for treason, for claiming to be a king.) In 1998 a statue of Bonhoeffer was unveiled by Queen Elizabeth II at Westminster Abbey, one of a group of ten Christian martyrs in the twentieth century.

(a) Find out exactly what the word 'martyr' means. What other religions remember their martyrs? Who are the other nine remembered at Westminster Abbey?

(b) Imagine! This letter about the statue appears in a newspaper

Dear Editor,
Much as I feel sorry that Pastor Bonhoeffer was executed only a few weeks before the war ended, he was not a martyr but a criminal. People who try to kill heads of state – or anyone else for that matter – can't be viewed as saints.
Yours sincerely ...

Write your reply to this letter to the newspaper.

7 Together with a friend, make a bullet point list using two columns for what makes Bonhoeffer like and unlike Guy Fawkes. You might need to use an encyclopaedia or web search to find out more about Guy Fawkes first. Do you find one item on your list more important than the others? Which one – and why?

8 Do this in threes! Two of you are the interrogators of Bonhoeffer. Script five key questions you would like to ask him. The third person – who must not see the questions in advance – uses the time to re-read about what Bonhoeffer did and knew in the plot. This person has to play the part of Bonhoeffer. Role-play the scene in front of the class. The audience has to decide how convincing the questions and the answers are.

9 Do this in pairs! Devise a code within an ordinary letter that Bonhoeffer might write to fellow plotters. In other words, it will read like an ordinary letter. Write your letter including the coded message. Then exchange letters with another pair and try to crack their code.

10 Design a badge or poster to illustrate an important quality you have chosen from Bonhoeffer's life (e.g. courage).

RMEP
A division of SCM-Canterbury Press Ltd
13–17 Long Lane, London EC1A 9PN

www.rmep.co.uk

Copyright © Terence Copley 2008

Terence Copley has asserted his right under the Copyright, Designs and Patents Act, 1988, to be identified as Author of this Work.

First published in 2008 by RMEP

A catalogue record for this book is available from the British Library

ISBN 978-1-85175-354-3

Photo acknowledgements: cover photograph, pp. 8, 10 (right), 17 and 19 © by Gütersloher Verlagshaus, Gütersloh, in der Verlagsgruppe Random House GmbH, München; p7 © Austrian Archies/ CORBIS; p10 (left) © Hulton-Deutsch Collection/CORBIS.

Designed and typeset by
TOPICS – The Creative Partnership, Exeter

Printed and bound in Great Britain by Halstan & Co. Ltd, Amersham

Notes for Teachers

Since the first *Faith in Action* books were published in the late 1970s, the series has developed to reflect changes in RE and now seeks to include a variety of faith perspectives. The style of the series has developed as well as the content. Emphasis is now placed on the pupils' own understanding, interpretation and evaluation of religious belief and practice and not just their knowledge of events. This is in line with changes in classroom RE over four decades, such as those embodied in the non-statutory *National Framework for RE* (2004) for England.

The *National Framework for RE* argues that RE should 'discuss and evaluate how religious beliefs and teachings inform answers to … ethical issues' and says that pupils should learn to 'evaluate the challenges and tensions of belonging to a religion' and 'evaluate their own and others' beliefs about world issues such as peace and conflict …' (page 28). Bonhoeffer contributes rich case study material towards these goals. The study of ethically oriented religious material can be good preparation for the Short Course GCSE RS and Ofsted argue that it can also motivate those boys who are underachieving in RE (*Making Sense of Religion*, 2007, page 15). The questions raised by Bonhoeffer's life, witness and work do not go away, especially that of whether violence can ever be justified on religious – and in his case, specifically Christian – grounds. Young people need to engage with these questions and consider what justice means in societies that have gone mad, if they are to be returned to sanity.

The Second World War ended more than 60 years ago. As the remaining survivors die away, Bonhoeffer's enduring legacy is likely to be not so much as an anti-Nazi rebel but as a person with a radical view of the Church, who saw Christian faith as a costly calling – much more than private beliefs and church attendance. He saw Christianity as a calling to become immersed in the worldliness of the world, with its complex problems, a world in which inaction always seems a tempting or at least excusable option. In our RE classrooms we should look towards the future as well as the past. Bonhoeffer prompts us to revisit uncomfortable issues in our time and – as a Yorkshire dialect saying puts it – to 'think on'.

TC 2008